P9-CLP-169

How to Build in the Country

·EDITED BY DONALD J. BERG·

◆ ◆ ◆

Ten Speed Press

Copyright 1986 by Donald J. Berg.
All rights reserved. No part of this book may be reproduced in any form, except for brief reviews, without the written permission of the publisher.

🖐️

TEN SPEED PRESS
P.O. Box 7123
Berkeley, CA 94707

Library of Congress Cataloging-in-Publication Data

How to build in the country.

Reprint. Originally published: Rockville Centre, N.Y. : Antiquity Reprints, © 1985
Includes index.
1. Country homes—Design and construction.
I. Berg, Donald.
TH4850.H67   1986   728.3'7   86-6053
ISBN 0-89815-182-1

Book and cover design by ANTIQUITY REPRINTS
Type set by John Moses/Modular Compart Graphics

Printed in the United States of America
1 2 3 4 5 — 90 89 88 87 86

About This Book

♦ ♦ ♦ ♦ ♦

The builders, architects and landscapers of last century's picture-perfect country homes left us a legacy of design ideas and practical building advice. Their words are as valuable now as they were when they were written.

I've selected some of the best hints, some that I've used myself and more that I wish I had, from nineteenth century builders' guides, farm journals and home and garden magazines. They're presented on the pages of this book in the original words of their authors. My own notes are in italics, like this. The book follows the normal building sequence from the original site plan through final planting and furnishing.

I hope you enjoy your reading and if you're dreaming of building a home in the country, that these hints are of some help. — Donald J. Berg

♦ ♦ ♦ ♦ ♦

CONTENTS

◆ ◆ ◆

FOREWORD

◆ ◆ ◆ ◆ ◆

Almost every American has an equally unaffected, though not, of course, an equally appreciative, love for "the country." This love appears intuitive, and the possibility of ease and a country place or suburban cottage, large or small, is a vision that gives a zest to the labors of industrious thousands. This one simple fact is of marked importance; it shows that there is an innate homage to the natural in contradistinction to the artificial—a preference for the works of God to the works of man; and no matter what passing influences may prevent the perfect working of this tendency, there it exists; and with all its town-bred incongruities and frequently absurd shortcomings, it furnishes a valuable proof of inherent good, true, and healthy taste.   ·

The great charm in the forms of natural landscape lies in its well-balanced irregularity. This is also the secret of success in every picturesque village, and in every picturesque garden, country-house, or cottage.

All previous experience in architecture is the inherited property of America, and should be taken every advantage of. Each beautiful thought, form, and mode that is not unsuited to the climate and the people, ought to be studied, sifted, and tested, its principles elucidated, and itself improved on; but the past should always be looked on as a servant, not as a master.

By Calvert Vaux, from his 1867 book, VILLAS & COTTAGES

◆ ◆ ◆ ◆ ◆

SELECTING & PLANNING YOUR PROPERTY

* * ◆ * *

FERGUSON ALB.

Don't Build in a Valley

❖ ❖ ◆ ❖ ❖

There are many beautiful, tempting, and, we may add, many really excellent sites in *valleys*. The soil is usually fertile, and the growth luxuriant. But the usual objections to narrow and deep valleys, where there is much water, are the dampness, and, often, the unhealthness, of the air there.

There is also another point worthy the consideration of our readers. This is the coldness in winter of all small or deep valleys, compared with the surrounding country. This, though not very perceptible to the senses, exerts a very important influence on vegetation. In a quiet winter night, the coldest air slides down into the bottoms of valleys, while the hills around are in a considerably higher temperature. Hence, many trees and plants will thrive on a higher level, which perish in a deep valley. We know a charming valley in Connecticut, where the peach and the cherry seldom perfect a crop of fruit, owing to the greater severity and prevalence of the frosts there, while they bear uniformly and well, in the adjacent country, on a higher level.

From HINTS TO PERSONS ABOUT BUILDING IN THE COUNTRY, 1847

Find a Waterside Site If You Can

Those valleys bordering on large pieces of water, which maintain a more uniform temperature than the land, afford admirable sites for building. Such are the valleys of large rivers and lakes, like the Hudson, and the great lakes in the State of New York. These broad sheets of water have such an effect in equalizing the temperature of the atmosphere for miles around them, that they usually add a month or more to the growing season on their banks. The frosts of Spring and Autumn are warded off, and crops of fruit are preserved, when they are destroyed in the interior of the country. On the banks of a large bay in the Hudson the spring is always ten days earlier, and the autumn ten days later, than in the same latitude thirty miles east or west. The shores of lakes Ontario, Erie, and the smaller lakes in this State, which do not freeze in winter, enjoy a still more marked exception from destructive frosts, as compared with the back districts of country unprotected by them. Every person choosing a site for a country residence, who is fond of his garden and orchard, will, therefore, when he has it in his power, give the preference to the borders of large rivers and lakes.

By A. J. Downing, from his HINTS TO PERSONS ABOUT BUILDING IN THE COUNTRY, 1847

Don't Build on Bad Soil

In choosing a position for the house itself, the character of the soil and sub-soil should receive attention. It is evident on a moment's reflection, that the worst soil is one naturally wet, and the best, one naturally dry. The site for a dwelling should never be selected where the sub-soil is naturally wet and springy, unless it is capable of being made perfectly dry by draining—because dampness of the house, and consequent unhealthiness of its inmates, almost inevitably follow the selection of such a situation. A good loam soil, on a gravelly sub-soil, is always an unexceptionable position for placing a house, as far as relates to this point. To those who desire fine ornamental grounds, or even fertile meadows and orchards (and we can hardly imagine the case of any country proprietor who does not), of course, attention to the *quality* of the soil immediately about the site of the house will not be overlooked. Though it is not impossible to render almost any soil fit for cultivation, yet it is infinitely wiser to chhose a site where nature had given the necessary conditions of good soil, rather than to undertake the great labor and ill-rewarded expense attending all considerable operations to change the character of soil.

From HINTS TO PERSONS ABOUT BUILDING IN THE COUNTRY, 1847

Where Should You Build?

♦ ♦ ♦ ♦ ♦

It very frequently occurs that circumstances compel us to build on a particular site, so that all choice is out of the question. But as there are annually a greater number of new localities selected and built upon in this country, than in any other, the opportunity of choosing where to build is open to a large majority of those who intend erecting a country dwelling in the United States.

The *best position* for a dwelling house, all other things being equal, it is almost unanimously agreed, is, for an irregular country, a *middle elevation*, half way between the low valleys and the high hills—open to the south and west, and sheltered from the north and east.

From HINTS TO PERSONS ABOUT BUILDING IN THE COUNTRY, 1847

Don't Build on Top of a Hill

The most *popular* sites, those usually chosen by inexperienced proprietors in the middle States, are the summits of hills of moderate elevation, overlooking extensive prospects. Now there are some advantages, but also very great disadvantages, in these high positions. The prominent advantages which such sites are supposed to possess are wide prospects, and conspicuousness for the dwelling itself: *to see*, and *to be seen*, to the greatest possible advantage. But every one having a cultivated taste for fine landscapes, must greatly prefer agreeable views, vistas or portions of trees with rich foreground, to wide panoramas of country. It is, in fact, the difference between a pictured landscape, and a geographical map. The *panorama* is striking and interesting, when seen occasionally, but it wants the interest, the home-like feeling of appropriation—which a view of moderate extent affords. As regards the ambition which is gratified with placing one's house where it may be a landmark for ten miles round, it is a false ambition which we have no sympathy with—a taste not in keeping with our social habits, and foreign to that equality of condition which all Americans are impatient of seeing greatly violated.

By A. J. Downing, from his HINTS TO PERSONS ABOUT BUILDING IN THE COUNTRY, 1847

The Difficulty of Hill·top Sites

From HINTS TO PERSONS ABOUT BUILDING IN THE COUNTRY, 1847

There are practical objections to sites upon the tops of hills, or high ridges, which are of great moment. The first of these is the great difficulty of raising all kinds of trees and shrubs in high and exposed sites. There are, apparently, but few persons aware that ornamental trees will advance twice as rapidly, the soil being the same, in a midway level, or a valley, as they will upon the summits of hills or high ridges. This is partly owing to the high winds, to which they are constantly exposed, and which render the annual growth of wood comparatively dwarfish, and partly to the greater dryness of the soil, which, in this climate, does not afford a continued supply of moisture to the roots.

But we may also add, as an offset to the grand prospect which these elevated sites afford, the labor of walking, riding, or driving up and down a long hill. If the road can be made gradual and easy this is not much, but in situations that we could name, where this is by no means the case, the daily effort (for there is no escape from it), of dragging up and down hill, becomes a burden, to be relieved of which, the proprietor would gladly exchange his wide-spread view for a more limited landscape, and an easier approach.

Set Your Home Away from the Road

◆ ◆ ◆ ◆ ◆

The building site is, of course, the first thing to be considered. One's first resolution regarding it should be to avoid all anxiety to jump into the road. A house crowding upon the highway loses all dignity and home-like repose, and gains nothing but dust. Such choice of location may possibly be an hereditary trait, coming down from that long ago time, when houses grew up along the faintly-marked trails of emigration, and closely clung there, as if in mortal fear of savages and wild animals lurking in the back-ground. But in these peaceful days, it is in better taste to sit back in a leisurely and composed way, as if not afraid of one's own fields and woodlands, but at home and happy with them. Let no site be chosen because of its proximity to the road, or because it is "handy to water." Select the finest spot on the farm—a place combining, if possible, elevation, eastern and southern frontage, natural trees, a pleasant outlook, and make all else conform to it.

By E. H. Leland, from his 1882 book, FARM COTTAGES

Planning Your Entry Drive

In a case that recently occurred near a country town at some distance from New York, a road was run through a very beautiful estate, one agreeable feature of which was a pretty though small pond that, even in the dryest seasons, was always full of water, and would have formed an agreeable adjunct to a country-seat. A single straight pencil-line on the plan doubtless marked out the direction of the road; and as this line happened to go straight through the pond, straight through the pond was the road accordingly carried, the owner of the estate personally superintending the operation, and thus spoiling his sheet of water, diminishing the value of his lands, and increasing expense by the cost of filling in, without any advantage whatever: for a winding road so laid out as to skirt the pond, would have been far more attractive and agreeable than the harsh, straight line that is now scored like a railway track clear through the undulating surface of the property; and such barbarisms are of constant occurrence. Points of this nature deserve the utmost attention, instead of the reckless disregard they generally meet with. When once a road is laid out, its fate is settled, and no alteration is likely to be made: it is, therefore, the more desirable that its direction should be well studied in the first instance.

By Calvert Vaux, from his 1867 book, VILLAS & COTTAGES

Which Way
Should You Face Your House?

The *aspect* of the dwelling should be considered in choosing a position. The fixed location of roads, rivers, or other important features in the scene, often lies in the way of a free choice in this particular. At the same time there are numberless instances in which we see great inattention to it, where there was no obstacle to its proper consideration.

The best aspect, in any country, for the principal front of a house, is that towards the *fair weather quarter*—that point of the compass from which the fairest and blandest wind blows most days in the year—and the worst aspect, that from which the greatest number of storms come.

Keeping these principles in view, it is evident that the *south-west* is the best aspect for the dwelling house in the United States, and the *north-east* the worst aspect. The longest, most numerous, and most disagreeable storms come from the last-named point of the compass, and the most delicious of our fair weather days are from what the Indians called the "sweet south-west," the land where their ideal heaven of hunting grounds lies.

By A. J. Downing, from the book, HINTS TO YOUNG ARCHITECTS, 1847

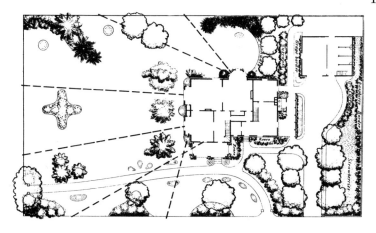

Sight Lines

♦ ♦ ♦ ♦ ♦

This landscape plan, from the 1870 book, SURBURBAN HOME GROUNDS, points out a simple consideration that's often overlooked in planning or landscaping modern homes. The dotted lines projecting from the house are sight lines. By drawing them, the designer can determine which views are allowed and which are blocked by his window placement or by the position of trees. By drawing similar lines, aimed at distant views, on your plot plan or survey, you'll be able to take best advantage of them. Don't forget that the process also works in reverse. Draw sight lines from your windows to anything you'd prefer not to see and you'll find the perfect spot for a hedge, a tree or a screen wall. — DJB

Don't Let this Happen to You!

Back in 1885, when this illustration was published in THE AMERICAN AGRICULTURIST, moving a country building was pretty easy. You'd have a Moving-Bee, invite all your friends and neighbors and their oxen and serve refreshments.

Today, things are a bit different. With concrete foundations, hookups to septic, plumbing and heating systems and utility wires to avoid, moving a home or barn can be a very expensive proposition. I'm told that it costs about half of what the construction of the building would be and I'll bet that there isn't a contractor in the country who'll take payment in cider and doughnuts.

When you've determined the ideal position for your home, have a surveyor draw it on your survey or plot plan to determine if it is within your property and zoning boundaries. Then, before you build, have him stake out the actual corners of the building on the ground. — DJB

SITE PLANS

◆ ◆ ◆ ◆

From the 1867 book,

COTTAGES AND FARM HOUSES

Plan for a 50' x 150' Lot

H— House; E— Entrance; O— Hot-beds; D— Dwarf fruit-trees; G— Grape trellis. The Vegetable Garden is made of four square plots.

♦ ♦ ♦ ♦ ♦

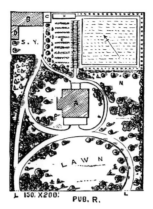

Plan for a 150' x 200' Lot

A— House; B— Stable; D— Henery; C— Manure Pit; SY—
Stable Yard; H— Hot-beds; G— Dwarf Fruit-trees; N—
Drying-yard; F— Rasberries, along one side of which is a
Grape Arbor covering the walk; L and L— Entrances.
Currants and other small fruits are planted around the
outside border.

◆ ◆ ◆

This garden has the appearance of a much larger place than
it really is; in fact, the plan could be applied to a place of ten
or more acres just as well as to a limited space. The most is
done to conceal the narrow limits, and leave one to guess
how far one may be from the end of it when one is no more
than ten feet from the well-concealed fence; at the same
time, all the secondary buildings, such as barns, stables, etc.,
are very close to the main house, though they are entirely out
of sight.

Plan for a 100'x 200' Lot

A— House; B— Stable; T— Turn in Yard; D— Hot-beds; H— Grape Arbor; F— Dwarf and standard fruit-trees; G— Entrance Gate. Small fruits form the outside border of the Vegetable Garden.

◆ ◆ ◆

In the plan, smoothly-curved walks are drawn in the thickets of large trees; there is also a vine arbor, which is a handsome ornament.

Plan for an Acre Lot

S— Stable and Barn; A— Greenhouse and Grapery; O— Double Henery; H— Hen Yard set with fruit-trees; D— Grape Arbor, between which and Greenhouse is a row of dwarf fruit-trees; I— Dwarf and Standard fruit-trees and currants; F— Fountain; J— Flowers; O— Water-closet and Garden Tool house; E— Dwarf fruit-trees.

◆ ◆ ◆ ◆ ◆

Plan for an Irregular Plot

A— House; S— Stable; at one end of which is a Hot-bed; O— Orchard.

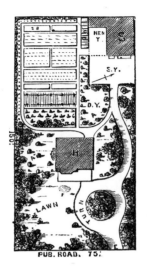

Plan for
a 75'x150' Lot

❖ ❖ ❖ ❖ ❖

H— House; S— Stable; A— Fruit-trees on Lawn; F— Flowers; DY— Drying-yard; SB— Strawberries on the four corners of the garden plot; HB— Hot-beds.

❖ ❖ ❖ ❖ ❖

Plan for a Five Acre Lot

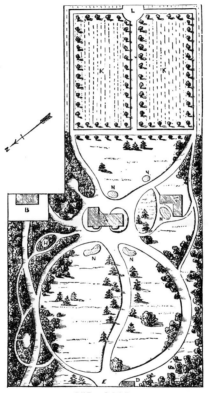

A— House; B— Coach-house, Stable, Yard; C— Greenhouse and Grapery; D— Gardener's Cottage; E— Principal Entrance; F— Entrance to Barn; H— Group of Rhododendrons and Azaleas; K— Kitchen Garden; L— Entrance; N— Flower beds. In this plan the Kitchen Garden occupies about one and a half acres.

Plan for a Two Acre Lot

♦ ♦ ♦ ♦ ♦

A— House, E— Entrance; B— Stables and Carriage House; D— Greenhouse and Grapery; I— Henery with double yard containing a few fruit-trees; SB— Strawberries; RB— Rasberries; V— Dwarf Orchard; O— Standard Orchard. Grapes are grown between the Greenhouse and Stables. The surrounding border of the Garden is set with Blackberries.

♦ ♦ ♦ ♦ ♦

HINTS ON HOME DESIGN

* * ◆ * *

An Object For Imitation

• • • • •

From the 1852 book, RURAL ARCHITECTURE

There are found in the older states many farm and country houses that are almost models, in their way, for convenience in the main purposes required of structures of their kind, and such as can hardly be altered for the better. Yet instead of standing as objects for imitation, they have been ruled out as antiquated, and unfit for modern builders to consult, who have in the introduction of some real improvements, also left out, or discarded much that is valuable, and, where true comfort is concerned, indispensable to perfect housekeeping. In the rage for innovation of all kinds, among much that is valuable, a great deal in house-building has been introduced that is absolutely pernicious. Take, for instance, some of our ancient-looking country houses of the last century, which, in America, we call old. See their ample dimensions; their heavy, massive walls; their low, comfortable ceilings; their high gables; sharp roofs; deep porches, and spreading eaves, and contrast them with the proportionless, and card-sided things of a modern date, and draw the comparison in true comfort, which the ancient mansion really affords, by the side of the other.

Good Design is a Good Investment

❖ ❖ ❖ ❖ ❖

Those who have watched the progress of Rural Architecture for some years past, have noticed a marked advance in architectural design and proportion and convenient and economical interior arrangement; yet, compared with the large number of structures yearly put up, the really attractive and tasteful buildings form the exception, and not the rule. Building, at best, is an expensive undertaking, and those who engage in it without availing themselves of the progressive improvements of the day, make investments from which it is difficult to realize first cost; while he who embraces the principles of beauty, harmony, good taste, etc., rarely fails to command his customer, and a handsome profit when ready to sell. The fact we desire to impress most thoroughly is, that it costs no more to build correctly and beautifully than to ignore all rules of taste, and that every one in this broad land who means to have a home of his own, should have a home worth owning.

From WOODWARD'S COTTAGES AND FARM HOUSES, 1867

How to Choose a Home Style

To harmonize with the surrounding scenery, to enter into the spirit of the landscape, is the highest beauty of a domestic building. This is too often overlooked;—and we find the dignity and repose of Nature broken by the presence of white, bare, bleak abodes, set ostentatiously in unplanted fields. Flat roofs and horizontal lines are opposed to the ascending lines of rocks and mountains around them; lofty turrets and steep gables rise up to contradict the natural expression of level plains. A house may be considered beautiful in the situation which suits it; its precise copy, in an unfit place, will always be a miserable deformity.

From THE REGISTER OF RURAL AFFAIRS, 1865

◆ ◆ ◆

The simplest rule for determining what style of building is best adapted to a particular kind of scenery, is to determine first the character of both the architecture and the landscape in question. Our own maxim is, that the bolder and more irregular the scenery, the bolder and more irregular the style of architecture it demands. Hence, building with highly varied outlines, with towers and the like, are most fittingly placed amid bold hills, and in a broken and mountainous country.

For a flat or level country, almost any simple style of building is in good keeping, Hence the propriety of the modifications of the cottage and villa forms which generally prevail there, and which are always pleasing when they express the simple life of the country gentleman, farmer, or proprietor of the soil—and equally unpleasing when they exhibit the finery of town houses, or ambitious architectural ornaments not properly answering to the habits or wants of their inhabitants.

From HINTS TO YOUNG ARCHITECTS, 1847

Common·sense Design is Always in Fashion

Fashion is not the synonym of taste; nor is beauty monopolized by wealth. A low log-cabin, nestled in the woods, the moss grown over its roof, the morning-glories climbing to the rustic window, is more attractive and is a better home than many a costly marble mansion. But the effort of "putting the best foot foremost," and anxiously attempting much display, costs our country homes the truth, the comfort, the sobriety which ought to characterize their architecture.

No house can fail to please whose form and hue accord with the adjacent country; which looks just what it is, neither less nor more; whose proportions and details are formed upon the principles of taste; and whose inner arrangement regards economy of space and gives attention to the laws of health,—requiring the fewest steps, presenting the greatest cheerfulness, neatness and convenience for common and daily use. All which the poorest man who builds can have as well as the rich; for Providence opens a short road to comfort, but hedges up the path to luxury.

From THE REGISTER OF RURAL AFFAIRS, 1865

Some Design Ideas

The site selected for the dwelling, and the character of the scenery and objects immediately surrounding it, should have a controlling influence upon the style in which the house is to be constructed. A fitness and harmony in all these is indispensable.

As a general remark, all buildings should show for themselves, what they are built of. Let stone be stone; bricks show on their own account; and of all things, put no counterfeit by way of plaster, stucco, or other false pretense other than paint, or a durable wash upon wood: it is a miserable affectation always, and of no possible use whatever.

From the 1852 book, RURAL ARCHITECTURE

♦ ♦ ♦

When we are considering a structure, as a whole, or in its parts, with reference to appearance and expression, rather than mere utility and comfort, a close adherence to right principles of design is peculiarly desirable. Although this will set aside many fanciful forms which are common and fashionable, there is no danger of its producing an unpleasing uniformity. While the surface and scenery of the country exhibit an unbounded diversity, and the condition, character, and tastes of our countrymen are almost as various, our architecture, if properly conformed to these, incurs no danger of tiring by its sameness.

From the 1856 book, VILLAGE & FARM COTTAGES

What Shape
Should Your New House Be?

All builders will agree that the most economical form in which a dwelling can be erected is a *cube*, because it contains more space within a given area of walls and roof than any other. Next to this is a parallelogram. The more irregular the outline of a building, the more the cost is increased, because it has more exterior surface, and therefore requires more wall or weather boarding, more roof, more gutters, and more fixtures and ornaments, when the house is in a handsome style.

On the other hand, the irregular form has great advantages, not only in the greater beauty of effect which the architect is enabled to bestow on it, but in its variety of sizes, forms, and consequently accommodation of its apartments within, as well as in the greater number and variety of views afforded without.

Hence, those who desire to combine as much economy as possible, with good taste in building a residence, will select a cube or rectangle for the outline of its ground plan; while those to whom expense is of less importance than convenience and picturesque effect, will adopt the irregular form.

From HINTS TO YOUNG ARCHITECTS, 1847

The Value of Simple Design

It is difficult to perceive, amid the glitter of ornament, the superior dignity and beauty of *simplicity*. We confess as hearty a love of decoration and ornament in architecture as any one. But it must be *consistent,* to satisfy us. It must express a beauty which pervades the building itself, everywhere, and not seem *patched on*, to catch the eye, and hide its defects. Harmonious proportions, a well ordered distribution of parts, excellent constructions, and *afterwards*, a suitable degree of decorations. Else it is like a poor book badly printed, yet richly bound and glittering with gold leaf.

◆ ◆ ◆

A simple, well-planned structure costs less to execute, for the accommodation obtained, than an ill-planned one; and the fact of its being agreeable and effective, or otherwise, does not depend on any ornament that may be superadded to the useful and necessary forms of which it is composed, but on the arrangement of those forms themselves, so that they may balance each other and suggest the pleasant ideas of harmonious proportion, fitness, and agreeable variety to the eye, and through the eye to the mind. All this is simply a matter of *study before* building, not of additional *cost in* building.

By Calvert Vaux, from his 1867 book, VILLAS & COTTAGES

Build for Your Climate

♦ ♦ ♦ ♦ ♦

It will be apparent, without special argument, that our choice of style in our country houses should be controlled essentially by the climate. In northern climate, the flat roof is objectionable. The hot summer sun will be more than likely to open the joints and seams of the flat roof, and the sudden shower coming down with the force of a tropical storm, will find its way through, sadly to the detriment of our ceilings, our stuccoes and frescoes, as well as to the comfort and the commendable equability of temper of those who suffer the invasion. The heavy winter snows, too, require a steep roof, from which they will readily dislodge themselves without injury.

And so in the interior arrangements of the house the provisions for heating and ventilation, for summer freedom and winter coziness, for domestic comfort and the exercise of the commendable grace of country hospitality, due regard must be had to the conditions of climate. There must be a proper adaptation to them, if we would secure satisfactory country homes.

From WOODWARD'S COTTAGES AND FARM HOUSES, 1867

Some Home Design Hints

From THE REGISTER OF RURAL AFFAIRS, 1858

◆ ◆ ◆ ◆ ◆

Proportion may be shown in the smallest cottage as well as in the most magnificent palace—and the former should be carefully designed as well as the latter. However small a building may be, let it never show an awkward conception, when a good form is more easily made than a bad one.

◆ ◆ ◆

A profusion of decoration, or "gingerbread work," so often seen, more commonly shows a want of true architectural taste than its presence.

◆ ◆ ◆

In all cases study beauty of form and proportion, and not ornament. Tasteful simplicity is better than fanciful complexity—as a statue in simple drapery is better than one bedizzened with feathers, ribbons, and unmeaning gewgaws.

Hints on Planning a Country Home

From *THE REGISTER OF RURAL AFFAIRS, 1857*

1.   Let the kitchen (the most important apartment) always be on a level with the principal floor—and for strong light and free ventilation, it should have, if possible, windows on opposite or nearly opposite sides.

2.   The pantry or dish-closet should be between the kitchen and dining-room, and easily accessible from both.

3.   There should be a set of *easy* stairs from the kitchen to the cellar, and also an outer set into the cellar for admitting barrels, &c.

4.   More attention should be given to the arrangement and convenient disposition of such rooms as are in constant use, than those but occasionally occupied. Hence the kitchen and living room should receive more attention on the ground of convenience, than the parlor.

5.   Every entrance, except to the kitchen, should be through some entry or hall, to prevent the abrupt ingress of cold air, and for proper seclusion.

6.   Let the entry or hall be near the center of the house, so that ready and convenient access may be had from it to the different rooms; and to prevent the too common evil of passing through one room to enter another.

7.   Place the stairs so that the landing shall be as near the center as may be practicable, for the reason given for the preceding rule.

8.   Let the partitions of the second floor stand over those of the lower, as nearly as may be, to secure firmness and solidity.

The Advantage of Steep Roofs

Nineteenth century homebuilders knew the advantages of steep roofs. Since they shed water and snow more quickly, they lasted longer. The space that a steep roof encloses is much more useable. The "Section" of a house, from the 1856 book, VILLAGE AND FARM COTTAGES, shows that although the entire second floor is below the line of the roof, it's still completely habitable. — DJB

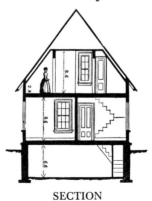

SECTION

A Country House Needs a Gable Roof

From THE REGISTER OF RURAL AFFAIRS, 1874

The ground plan of this design is so nearly square that those who prefer the four-sided or square roof can adopt it. I must confess, however, to a strong objection to such a roof on a house fairly in the country. It seems to look well enough in town or suburb, but the upper horizontal line of the span roof, with its handsome gables, will generally afford the beholder most pleasure, and appears to harmonize best with country scenery. There is also a practical reason for it worth considering. The good housewife prizes a fine, open garret for many purposes. Not the least of these is having a place for drying clothes in cold or stormy weather, where they can hang regardless of thieves or sudden rain, until she is ready to iron them. This is a principal reason why at least one wing of some of the other designs is carried up two stories when good proportion in so narrow a building seems to require less height. The roofs also are pretty steep, allowing snow and rain to slip off easily, making the roof more durable, beside giving better head room.

This also is rather in violation of what is usually taught in architectural works, for there we are apt to find the flattest roofs on two-story houses. The idea appears to be that the house with steep roof, being actually higher, must necessarily *appear* so. This I believe to be a mistake, at least on rather narrow buildings. Having given particular attention to the subject for some time past, and made many comparisons, it is found that houses with flattish roofs invariably look higher than their steeper roofed neighbors. It would appear that we judge mainly by apparent height of the sides, or distance from side eaves to the ground.

The Entry

From the 1882 book, FARM COTTAGES

If one's house must be small and the rooms few, still a hall or some sort of pleasant vestibule ought to be afforded, rather than have the living-room or parlor open abruptly into the open air. It is good for family habits, too, that the children have a regular place for hats and caps, and an opportunity before a hall mirror to see that they are presentable prior to appearing in the sitting or dining-room. Such little household regulations teach children order and self-control.

This moral view of the Hall brings up another consideration. There are many kind-hearted, fair-minded house-keepers who regard the main entrance of their houses as being too sacred for daily use, and prefer that husband and children and intimate friends should "run around" to a side or a kitchen door. This is a mistake. Better live in a hut with but one entrance than have a door-way too grand for those nearest us to walk through!

But these same fair-minded house-keepers will exclaim, "Oh, it is all very well to talk about the footsteps of those nearest us, but I can't afford to have my hall-carpet covered with mud every day and torn to tatters in six months!"

Of course you cannot afford it, nor can you afford to have your children acquire the careless manners and habits that come of the back-door principle. Have a door-mat at the hall door, and teach little feet to respect it.

A Design Idea

Are you building a home at the seaside or in rolling country? There's probably a view that would be much more dramatic from the second floor. This 1867 cottage by George E. Harney shows one way of taking advantage of the vista. By building the roof of the entry porch higher and using the space created as an open balcony, the architect captured views and cool night breezes. In winter, storm windows change the space into a "conservatory," a sunny, protected spot for potted plants that wouldn't survive the cold. DJB

Avoid North Entrances

◆ ◆ ◆ ◆ ◆

A due north aspect is a very objectionable one for a country house, not only on account of the bad weather to which it exposes the principal side of the house, but also because of the accumulation of snow and ice about it in winter, rendering it far more difficult to keep it in hospitable order than a house with a warm southern entrance front.

For a country house which is only intended for summer use, the owner of which leaves it for town in winter, this is not a valid objection. Indeed, a northern entrance is, in our mid-summer, more agreeable, perhaps, than a southern one—its piazzas always cool, and its view opening upon the best and brightest face of the lawn and trees—that turned towards the sun. But the comparatively short season to which this can, in our latitude, be applied with truth, renders a northern aspect a very objectionable one for families residing in the country during the whole year.

By A. J. Downing, from the book, HINTS TO YOUNG ARCHITECTS, 1847

Do You Need a Parlor?

The windows and Venetian blinds are tightly closed, the door is tightly shut, and the best room, that I am now thinking of, is, in consequence, always ready for—what? for daily use? Oh, no; it is in every way too good for that. For weekly use? No, not even for that—but for *company* use; and thus the choice room with the pretty view, is sacrificed, to keep up a conventional show of finery that pleases no one, and is a great, though unacknowledged, bore to the proprietors. Such is one style of best parlor to be found in America; and though it is by no means universal, it is far too general for comfort. A drawingroom like this becomes a sort of quarantine in which to put each plague of a visitor that calls; and one almost expects to see the lady of the house walk in with a bottle of camphor in her hand, to prevent infection, she seems to have such a fear that any one should step within the bounds of her real every-day home life. All this is absurd. No room in any house, except, perhaps, in a very large mansion, ought to be set apart for company use only. If a reception-room for strangers is needed, it should be a small, unpretending room, certainly not the most agreeably situated apartment in the house, *which should be enjoyed daily*, for it is not the having any good thing, but the using it, that gives it its value.

From the 1867 book, VILLAS & COTTAGES

A Common Kitchen

• • • • •

The Advantage of a Small Kitchen

Kitchens should be *too* small for setting a table, and if there is any probability of undertaking such a thing, they should be still smaller. If there is any one thing better calculated than another to weaken digestion, mar the pleasure of eating, grate upon delicate nerves, and harrow up the feelings generally of persons of some degree of culture and refinement, it is to sit down to meals in a room impregnated with the odors of cooking, with stove close at hand containing steaming pots and boilers of turnip, cabbage or potato water, and the greasy liquid in which meat or fish was cooked; on the other side perhaps a shelf or sink, containing the endless list that will accumulate in cooking, of dirty dishes, pans, spiders, skillets, griddle greasers, and what not, that in the hurry to have the meal at the exact minute, must be tossed into the nearest catch-all. Oh, what a place for that social and intellectual feast—that warm commingling of the feelings and affections which in some families can occur only at meal time, as then only will all the members be together—even family worship will probably be conducted here! Is this picture too strong? *"You* don't have things so." Perhaps not. But others must admit, at least to themselves, that it may be even worse.

From THE REGISTER OF RURAL AFFAIRS, 1873

Good Advice

• • ◆ • •

There is nothing more essential to the comfort, and consequently to the happiness, of the family, than that the dining-room should be, of all the apartments of the house, the most pleasant and the most attractive. And, to this end, the first requisite is, that it should be properly placed. In building, or in the occupation of the residence already constructed, let that room be selected for the purpose into which the morning sun at least shall throw its cheerful rays. In a cold climate, at no time is its presence more welcome than at the breakfast-table. If practicable, let both the morning and evening sunlight illuminate the room. These points can be attained by the choice of the southeastern exposure.

From the 1867 book, COTTAGES AND FARM HOUSES

Attic Bedrooms

◆ ◆ ◆ ◆ ◆

Attic bedrooms may be so planned as to afford a valuable addition to the accommodation of a country house. A more extended view is generally to be obtained from these rooms than from the rest of the house, and as they may be made quite as comfortable, though not, of course, so symmetrical, as the second floor chambers, they deserve a fair share of consideration; and the economical advantages they offer have frequently led me, in practice, to advise the use of a high-pitched roof. The acute angle of the roof precludes the possibility of any large surface being exposed to the vertical rays of the sun, and the flat on the top, being furred down some three or four feet, supplies an air-chamber above the attic ceiling that acts as a satisfactory shield from the heat.

By Calvert Vaux, from his 1867 book, VILLAS & COTTAGES

◆ ◆ ◆ ◆ ◆

The attic in the peak of the roof above the upper rooms should be ventilated so as to secure a circulation of air—an important precaution for houses built in warm climates.

From the 1897 book, HOW TO BUILD A HOME

GOOD DETAILS

❖ ❖ ❖ ❖ ❖

A Country House Needs a Porch

♦ ♦ ◆ ♦ ♦

A country house without a porch is like a man without an eyebrow; it gives expression, and gives expression where you most want it. The least office of a porch is that of affording protection against the rain-beat and sun-beat. It is an interpreter of character; it humanizes bald walls and windows; it emphasizes architectural tone; it gives hint of hospitality; it is a hand stretched out (figuratively and lumberingly, often) from the world within to the world without.

By Donald G. Mitchel, from his 1867 book, RURAL STUDIES

♦ ♦ ♦

VERANDAS are most desirable on the south and west sides of a house, for while they ward off the mid-day heat of summer, they still freely admit the low down winter sun.

From the 1882 book, FARM COTTAGES

An Arbor·Veranda

From the book THE ARCHITECTURE OF COUNTRY HOUSES, 1852

◆ ◆ ◆ ◆

To build a substantial roof with a veranda round the whole cottage, or round three sides of it, would be too expensive an outlay for most occupants of such a dwelling. This arbor, which is barely the skeleton of such a veranda—being, in fact, only an arbor with rather better posts than usual, would cost but little, and would not only be productive of much beauty, but a good deal of profit. We suppose it to be covered with those two best and hardiest of our native *grapes*—the Isabella and Catawba—the most luxuriant growers in all soils—affording the finest shade, and, in the middle and western States, giving large and regular crops of excellent fruit.

Window Hoods

From the 1867 book, VILLAS & COTTAGES

Hoods to windows in American country houses are features that seem to spring naturally from the peculiarities of the climate, and the needs they give rise to. The upper sashes of windows with hoods can always be left a little open without any chance of the rain beating in; and even when of small size they protect the glass from the direct vertical rays of the summer sun, and receive the first blows from the winter storm. They also add much to the artistic effect of a rural building.

It is to be observed that, in summer, a small window is in one respect most comfortable, as a wall is a better protection from heat than glass or Venetian blinds. But, on the other hand, large windows are desirable to throw open for the summer evening breeze, and to let in planty of cheerful iight during dull winter and spring days. The hood, in a measure, connects these two opposite needs. A veranda all round a house is delightful for a month or two in the heat of summer; but most healthily-constituted persons like to have the opportunity to admit a stream of glorious, warm, genial sunlight into their rooms whenever they feel inclined to enjoy it, and this can not be obtained if the veranda entirely encircles the living apartments. The hood, on the other hand, defends the window from the powerful rays of the mid-day sun without shutting it out entirely.

Country Home Details

From the 1867 book, VILLAS & COTTAGES

The *veranda* is perhaps the most specially American feature in a country house; nothing can compensate for its absence, and endless opportunities for variety in design occur in treating this part of a country house.

The *bay-window* is the peculiar feature next to the veranda that an American rural home loves to indulge in. There can, indeed, scarcely be too many for the comfort of the house, or too few for the comfort of the purse, for I regret to add that they are expensive features. The simplest form is a plain semi-octagon, with simple shed-roof, shown above. This sort of bay is very commonly finished with a roof running up to a point against the wall; but the effect thus produced is always mean and disagreeable, and a straight line for some distance, as shown on the sketch, gives the appearance of the windows *belonging* to the house much more than the other mode.

The *balcony* is a feature that can now and then be introduced to advantage; and a specimen that tells the whole story, and scarcely needs any further detail, is shown in the illustration.

Dormer-windows are of several sorts, according to the style of the house. They are often made *too small,* and considerable comfort and effect is thereby lost, for a small one costs very nearly as much as a large one, and is not half so available. A dormer is a capital feature in a country house.

◆ ◆ ◆ Closets ◆ ◆ ◆

Closets are indispensable for comfort, and should be numerous. It is safe to assume that it is wise to sacrifice floor-space of rooms for closets, for they secure not only comfort, but order and neatness in the appearance of the house. The specifications should name the height and width of shelves, distance between them, size and arrangement of drawers, and should require hooks for hanging, which will cost little more if of brass or bronze instead of iron, and should be double. The door should not swing into a closet, thus doing away with half the hanging room, to say nothing of injury to the contents; and yet this is a common fault with some architects and builders. Examine the plans to see that the hooks in closets for hanging clothing are at the proper height from the floor, and that the shelves above the hooks start at a sufficient height above them to give room for removing garments. Any practical housekeeper will say that "a house cannot have too many closets."

From HOW TO BUILD A HOME,   1897

◆ ◆ ◆ Doors ◆ ◆ ◆

Doors are generally hung according to the sweet will of the carpenter, but there are two ways to hand a door, one so as to expose the room, the other so as to screen it. The first may be good for the more public rooms, but, in regard to bed-rooms, the doors must swing so that, when partly open, they will shield the apartment from view. Closet doors should be hung so that the closet may receive light from the nearest window. Doors are sometimes made to swing out on stair landings or halls, and who has not seen two doors so placed that they strike each other when opened? It is hardly necessary to say that these methods should not be adopted.

From the 1884 book, COTTAGES OR HINTS ON ECONOMICAL BUILDING

◆ ◆ ◆ ◆ ◆

Where economy is necessary, doors and windows should be what are called "stock" sizes, i.e., the regular sizes made by the mills of the vicinity in which the dwelling is to be located. To specify them will save the expense inseparable from unusual or irregular sizes. If, however, the house is so located as to have a fine view, it will be mistaken economy not to have one or more of the prominent windows wider.

From HOW TO BUILD A HOME, 1897

Let the Sun In

By E. H. Leland, from his 1882 book, FARM COTTAGES

The sun, if you will only open your house to him, is a faithful physician, who will be pretty constant in attendance, and who will send in no bills. Many years ago glass was something of a luxury, but now we can all have good-sized windows, and plenty of them, at moderate cost, and there is no excuse for making mere loop-holes, through which the sun can cast out half an eye, and from which one can gain only narrow glimpses of the beautiful outer world.

I am sufficiently acquainted with the conservative character of many country people to know that expressions of disdain will come from some quarters when I mention Bay Windows. Nevertheless bay windows are a good thing. Their effect is very much like letting heaven into one's house, at least it ought to be like that, for it is nothing but absurdity and wickedness to darken such windows with shutters or heavy curtains until only a struggling ray of sunlight can be seen.

The
Country Fireplace

◆ ◆ ◆ ◆ ◆

What we consider indispensable in a country house, be it large or small, is an old fashioned open fire-place, for burning wood on the hearth, if wood can be had, or, if not, coal in the grate, and, besides, for purposes of ventilation. We think, for practical reasons, the old poetic sentiment of the family fireside and the blazing log should not be lost sight of, and there should be at least one room in every house—the room that is the most used by the family as a sitting-room—made attractive and healthy by this means.

◆ ◆ ◆ ◆ ◆

From WOODWARD'S COTTAGES AND FARM HOUSES, 1867

Hints on Laying·out a Staircase

• • • • •

From THE REGISTER OF RURAL AFFAIRS, 1873

Who has not felt discouraged when standing at the foot of a long, straight flight of steps, looking up at that top which must be reached, however tedious and difficult the way may appear?

Put in a landing half or two-thirds up, and a turn in some other direction, and all is changed. The distant goal is hid, as in the journey of life, not seeing very far ahead, we start with confidence, rest a moment perhaps, or change the motion at the turn and reach the top as it were by two efforts, neither of which has been fatiguing. I speak with the more confidence of this matter, as the house we have occupied for years has such a landing, and the ease with which we reach the rooms above is still cause of congratulation, especially after a recent experience in climbing a straight flight. Probably as good proportion as any for steps is 7½ inch riser and 10 inch step. Make the top of second floor exactly 10 feet above the upper side of lower floor, and fifteen of these steps or sixteen risers will land you all right. It is important to make this close calculation before laying the joists, as a single step differing from the rest in height, if only by the fraction of an inch, is exceedingly annoying, and many a serious bruise has been brought about in this way, with perhaps not a suspicion of the cause.

A Substitute for Bay Windows

◆ ◆ ◆ ◆ ◆

If bay windows are too expensive, a very desirable substitute can be had by placing two ordinary sized windows side by side with a wide capacious ledge at the bottom for seats or for plants.

A room with a window like this cannot fail to be cheery, and its effect in a simple cottage house is quite sumptuous. There is likewise in its favor the fact that it is less exposed than the deep bay window to outer heat and cold.

In a kitchen or in a child's bedroom, or in an attic where the walls are low, two half-windows set side by side and made to slide or to open on hinges, admit a broad, generous light, and give an apartment a pretty and pleasing rustic air.

In the country, with a whole sky to draw from, let there be light! If any rooms in the house must look solely to the north for illumination, let them be the parlor and the spare chamber. People who come and go can be cheerful for a while in a north-windowed apartment, but the constant dwellers in a house need its sunniest rooms.

By E. H. Leland, from his 1882 book, FARM COTTAGES

Details That Keep a House Dry

* * * *

This cottage, from the 1850 book, THE ARCHITECTURE OF COUNTRY HOUSES, is a model of how a house can be designed to keep itself dry. The simple, sloping roof projects broadly to carry rain and snow away from the walls. The hoods over the windows protect them, even if they're left open at the top. The horizontal band of wood, just above the foundation, is a "water-table." It is beveled away from the house to carry off any water that runs down the walls. As you can see, the first floor is built two steps above the ground which is also terraced around the house. Water would have to climb up hill to get in. — DJB

YESTERDAY'S COUNTRY DESIGNS

• • • • •

It is our intention, in presenting a number of designs for country houses, to show what can be done with simple means, and to give sketches of cottages that may meet the wants of many who desire inexpensive homes which shall be at the same time cosy and picturesque.

It must be stated, however, that all we can hope to do in the compass of this little volume is to give some hints on building and offer a few suggestions and ideas which may be of value to those about to build. It is by no means claimed that the drawings here given are sufficient for constructing the houses. Proper working drawings are a much more serious affair, and should in all cases be prepared by an architect. This is as important for a cottage as for a mansion.

From the 1884 book, COTTAGES OR HINTS ON ECONOMICAL BUILDING

A Farm House

From THE REGISTER OF RURAL AFFAIRS, 1857

This design is intended for a farm-house, where the entire outlay is devoted to convenience and comfort, and not a dollar to mere ornament. It has a special regard to furnishing the greatest amount of room at the least practicable cost for a substantial erection, the whole being afforded for fifteen to seventeen hundred dollars.

It will be observed the rooms are compactly disposed, so that those required in connection, are very easily accessible to each other, and no space is lost. The dining room is long and narrow, the most economical form for such an apartment; the kitchen projects in part from the main building, so as to secure a current of air through the opposite doors. The pantry being placed between them, is readily accessible to both, and also affords a passage from one to the other.

A Hillside House

There are quite a few advantages to building a home into the side of a hill. The natural flow of rain water downhill and breezes uphill will keep it cooler and dryer. Simply adding large windows to the half exposed foundation walls will make bright and airy living space where a basement would have been. Rooms on the lower level, protected by the earth of the hill will be warmer in winter and cooler in summer.

The hillside house shown is from the 1856 book, VILLAGE AND FARM COTTAGES. — DJB

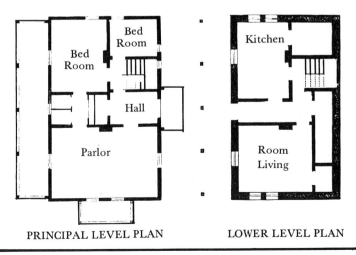

PRINCIPAL LEVEL PLAN   LOWER LEVEL PLAN

A Converted Coach·house

This cottage, from the 1856 book, VILLAGE AND FARM COTTAGES, was converted from an old coach-house. The 20'x20' floor area is just about the same as a modern two-car garage. The owner built a new steep roof to provide a second floor with useable space, then added the partitions, windows, doors and verandah that you see. The term, "Living Room," in the 19th century, simply meant the room in which the family spent most of their time. In this design, it's a combination kitchen and dining room. — DJB

Plan

A Country House

From THE REGISTER OF RURAL AFFAIRS, 1873

This plan needs little explanation. We go down cellar from the pantry, which is large enough to admit of a meal chest in the corner, or what is preferred by some, a closet 2½ feet high by 1 foot by 9 inches in depth, in the clear, with broad kneading-board hung on hinges for top. In this is a barrel of flour, and all the necessary aids to baking on narrower shelves close above. In this and some other plans the living-room is at the rear. This being the apartment most occupied by the family, every means should be used to make it pleasant. *Sunshine,* especially in winter, adds greatly to the cheerfulness of a home room; but houses often front northward, with nothing but a common highway in the foreground, while a beautiful view may open out from the rear.

Designs with living-rooms back are intended for such situations. The width and height of the verandas can be so managed as to keep out most of the sunshine in summer, while the sun, running lower in winter, will pour in his then welcome beams, streaking the carpet with gold, and lighting up the wood-work and furniture. How immeasurably better will a meal look and taste in such a room!

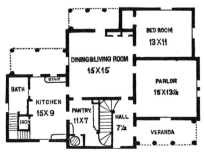

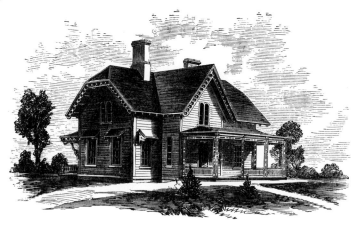

A Southern Home

♦ ♦ ♦ ♦

Any home built in a warm climate or for use as a summer house should be designed to keep itself cool. This 1876 cottage, by architect Isaac H. Hobbs, shows some of the best methods. Porches, window hoods and deep roof overhangs provide shade and allow the windows to remain open in a cooling rain. The kitchen, where most heat is generated, is separate from the main body of the house. Warm air from it, and from all of the other rooms in the house, can be vented through the upper level windows of the entry hall. — DJB

FIRST FLOOR PLAN   SECOND FLOOR PLAN

A Country Cottage

By A. J. Downing, from THE HORTICULTURIST
1847

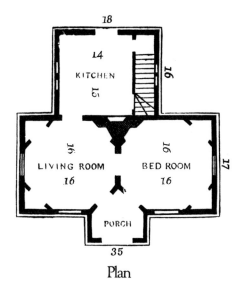

Plan

PRINCIPAL FLOOR.

A Simple House

From THE REGISTER OF RURAL AFFAIRS, 1857

This design which represents a house in a nearly square form, gives ten rooms within story and a half walls, the whole measuring only thirty by thirty-five feet inside. The rooms are probably as compactly arranged as can be possibly effected, not a single inch of the enclosed space being lost. The entry, 5 by 7 feet, conducts to the parlor on one side and to the dining-room on the other, the latter being also intended as the family or living-room. The stairs being flanked with plastered walls, made at one-fourth the expense required where open on one side with railing or balustrade. The entrance to the cellar from the kitchen is under these stairs.

The exterior conveys an expression of cheerfulness and neatness; and has so small an amount of ornamental appendages, that the cost is scarcely increased by them. The window under the small front gable, inserted for lighting the upper hall and stairs, imparts a certain sheltered aspect, which is carried out by the addition of the window hoods over the lower windows.

A Country House

THE HORTICULTURIST
1847

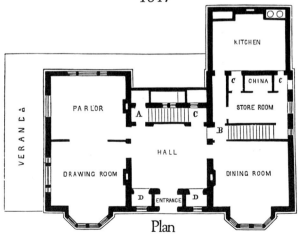

Plan

A Carriage·house

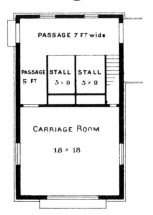

This combination stable/carriage house, designed by architect George E. Harney, in 1870, could be the model for an efficient garage and tool room today. As with most 19th century out-buildings, it was probably designed to comple-ment the owner's house with the same roof lines and similar materials and colors. The cupola was decorative but it also vented the building to keep it cool and dry. — DJB

An Outbuilding

◆ ◆ ◆

This little building, designed in 1867 by architect George E. Woodward, was described by him as a "tool-house, etc." Besides being thankful that we no longer need an outdoor "etc.", we can learn something from the design. The gingerbread, arched window and roof treatment that you see were a reflection of the same details on the main house. Last century's homeowners knew that by repeating the colors, materials and details of their home on fences and outbuildings, they made the home seem more a part of the land that it was on and improved the look of both. — DJB

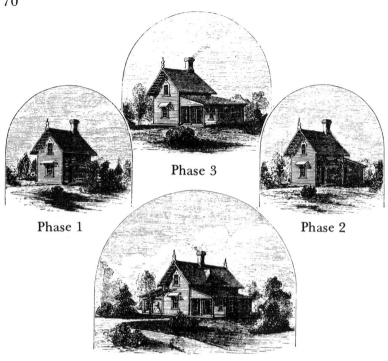

Phase 3

Phase 1

Phase 2

THE FINISHED HOUSE

Build a Little at a Time

It was common practice in the past to build small and to add rooms as needed. This design, from the 1867 book WOOD-WARD'S ARCHITECTURE AND RURAL ART, shows how it should be done. The finished house was envisioned from the start. The second floor, staircase, chimney and entry door were built first to remain through all the changes. New rooms were built on the outside of the old structure and passage doors replaced windows. With careful planning of the new construction, family life was disturbed as little as possible. — DJB

◆ ◆ ◆ ◆ ◆

HINTS ON HOME PLANS

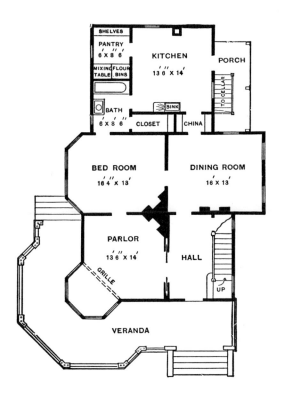

Hints on Home Plans

A well-studied plan is characterized by compactness and the absence of any visible make-shifts or after-thoughts. Everything fits well and seems in its natural place.

A rectangular house is the cheapest and best, the octagonal and circular forms are better adapted for bays or projections only. Very irregular and straggling plans may product picturesque results, but are sure to be comparatively expensive. A square house has always been a favorite with many practical-minded people. It is such a "sensible" shape and cuts up well into rooms. True, a given length of line, as a square, encloses a greater area than in any other rectangular form, so we get the most house for our materials and money. Still, we will probably find that, after arranging our plan, considering comfort and convenience alone, it will not result in a mathematical square; but, if it be compact and capable of being simply roofed, we need not reproach ourselves with undue extravagance.

All space occupied in passages and corridors, increasing the size but not the capacity of the building, is wasted.

Light and air are, we know, essentials of life. Let us not forget it in planning our house. Dark passages and stairways should not be tolerated.

From the 1884 book, COTTAGES OR HINTS ON ECONOMICAL BUILDING

How to Choose a Good Home Plan

A common mode of procuring a design is to take as a model some house already built. This particularly suits those who experience difficulty in understanding architectural drawings, and in forming the conception of an object, not actually before their eyes. To the copying of a pattern house, if one in all respects suitable can be found, there is perhaps no serious objection, except the sameness. But it is often forgotten that the house which exactly suits its present location and occupants, may seem quite out of place in some other situation, and may be wholly unfit for a different kind of family. If, as often happens, an attempt be made to modify it by altering its proportions, by curtailment in one part, or by some incongruous addition in another, the probability is that the good qualities of the original will be mostly lost, while their few remaining traces will only show the deformity of the alterations.

The same caution is applicable to the selection of published designs. Those principles which should direct in the formation of an original design ought also to control in some degree, at least, the choice of a ready-made plan.

From the 1856 book, VILLAGE & FARM COTTAGES

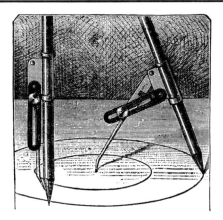

Hints on House Plans
From the 1897 book, HOW TO BUILD A HOME

In planning windows and doors to bedrooms, regard should be had to the importance of locating bedsteads and bureaus with reference to light and drafts, and windows should be arranged accordingly. It is sometimes discovered that the windows have been so injudiciously planned that there is no place for a bed to stand.

An easy way of planning for bedsteads, bureaus, etc., in rooms, is to cut pieces of cardboard of the proper size according to the scale of the rooms. This is usually one fourth inch to the foot. These pieces of card of the exact size of bedsteads, bureaus, buffets, etc., can be moved about on the architect's floor-plan of each room to determine the location of windows, doors, gas-brackets, etc.

◆ ◆ ◆

Whatever the plan adopted, let it, when once fixed on, be firmly adhered to. Even though it should be found in some slight degree imperfect, attempts to improve it after the work has begun will be more likely to result in injury, loss, and vexation, than in benefit. Those who adopt a published design with the idea of modifying it, should remember that a slight alteration may change its whole character, and destroy its value. Such a change can be safely made only in the same spirit as that which governed in the original formation; and to do it well requires at least equal skill.

Build on Paper First

It is a great thing to build the house that is to be one's home. There are few pleasures so unalloyed as that of selecting the ground, laying the foundation, and watching day by day the growth of wall and roof that go to form one's own secure kingdom through the years to come. And it is a pleasure that cannot be entered upon too seriously. If there are to be but three rooms, they will constitute the home, and the opportunity exists to make them either charmingly cozy and cheerful, or depressingly ugly. Therefore, even a small house-plan should be well considered. A house-plan is easily torn down and remodelled; it costs nothing to add a paper window here, or to remove a paper partition there; a pencil line changes a staircase or enlarges the dining-room; a few moments of inexpensive reflection lets the morning sunlight into a cheerless kitchen, builds a clothes-press, and remodels the pantry; or, if something better is thought of, the whole establishment can be easily tossed aside, and not even the shadow of the house-mover's bill presents itself. But, having put a plan into solid timber and mortar, and then coming to find how greatly the house might be improved—ah, woe the day! It is no idle thing to meddle with the stair-cases and partitions, and the gloomily-lighted kitchen.

From the 1882 book, FARM COTTAGES

Do You Understand Your House Plans?

◆ ◆ ◆ ◆ ◆

If you are not familiar with all the details of the house you propose to build, make yourself so, by a repeated examination of existing specimens, in dwellings in the same style, already erected. Above all, do not be satisfied by the mere expression on the plan, in figures, of the sizes of your rooms; but ascertain if the size is exactly what you suppose, and what you want, by looking at rooms already built of that size. Otherwise you may find to your regret, when it is too late, that "parlor 16 by 20" means something a great deal smaller, when actually enclosed within four walls, than it did in the air castle of your imagination, which you conjured up with the aid of your paper plans.

By A. J. Downing, from his HINTS TO PERSONS ABOUT BUILDING IN THE COUNTRY, 1847

TODAY'S COUNTRY DESIGNS

◆ ◆ ◆ ◆ ◆

Homestead Designs' KINGSTON

Just as yesterday's country builders could page through "pattern" books for plans of their ideal home, you might find just the home you want on the pages of a mail-order plan catalog. You'll find some of the best, combining traditional design with modern layouts and offering complete construction plans, on the next few pages. — DJB

◆ ◆ ◆ ◆ ◆

© R.S. OATMAN
1978

The Golden Age of Victorian Architecture

Architect Russell Swinton Oatman has reproduced twelve authentic 19th century homes for his catalog, THE GOLDEN AGE OF VICTORIAN ARCHITECTURE. Many, like the "Small Bracketed Cottage" shown, were designed as country homes. The original of this design, as shown below, first appeared in A. J. Downing's 1850 book, THE ARCHITEC- TURE OF COUNTRY HOUSES. For a copy of the catalog, send $5.00 to Russell Swinton Oatman, 132 Mirick Road, Princeton, MA 01541. Mr. Oatman has also applied his talent for accurate detailing to earlier period houses in his catalogs, THE NEW ENGLAND COLLECTION OF HOMES ($5.00), THE CAPE COD COLLECTION OF HOMES ($5.00), and THE OLD STURBRIDGE VILLAGE COLLECTION OF HOMES ($6.00). – DJB

Old Colonial Houses

An 18th Century Salt-Box

Architect Evan Pollitt traveled through New England and selected 52 historic homes for his catalogs, OLD COLONIAL HOMES and OLD CAPE COD HOUSES. He measured the exteriors and reproduced them authentically, then adapted the interiors for modern use and prepared complete construction plans that you can order. His catalogs offer brief histories of many of the homes and fascinating "then" and "now" illustrations of his designs. Write to: Even Pollitt, A.I.A., 61 Vista Drive, Easton, CT 06612 and enclose $5.00 for each catalog. — DJB

Evan Pollitt's Design #89

Copyright — The New Victorians Inc.

New Victorians

• • • • •

Kenneth Trumble hasn't reproduced historic houses for his series of twelve "New Victorians," but rather designed new homes inspired by the past. They have many of the details that you'll be looking for in a country home (deep roof overhangs; ample verandas and bay windows), combined with modern layouts and energy-efficient design. Many of the designs boast a variety of wood textures on the exterior; — coat them with a "weathering gray" stain and allow vines to climb the veranda posts and trellises and you'll have a timeless country home. — DJB

For a catalog, send $6.00 to The New Victorians, Inc., of Arizona, P.O. Box 32505, Phoenix, AZ 85064.

• • • • •

The KINGSTON, reversed or "mirrored"

Homestead Designs

Unlike some of the other plan services that I've mentioned, Homestead Designs hasn't attempted to reproduce historic designs in their homes, barns and garages. Instead, they've designed new homes that seem traditional because they combine the traditional values of simplicity, good proportions and flexibility. Many of the homes are designed to expand and alternate layouts are offered. Reversed plans are available — hold the plan you like up to a mirror and see if it will fit your site better that way. Send $3.00 to Homestead Design, P.O. Box 988, Friday Harbor, WA 98250 for their latest catalog. — DJB

Copyright — Country Designs

Country Designs

This barn/stable is just one of 32 country buildings available from Country Designs, P.O. Box 774, Essex, CT 06426, and featured in their $3.00 catalog. They have designs for stables, sheds, barns, garages, cottages and garden buildings. The practical layouts, good proportions and common-sense detailing of all of the buildings rival the best of yesterday's design. — DJB

Sun Designs' SENTINEL Gazebo

Sun Designs

No country landscape is finished without its complement of garden structures. Sun Designs has a variety of well detailed plans for gazebos, well houses, arbors, bird houses, bridges, sheds, small barns, dog houses, garbage can enclosures and even out-houses in a series of beautifully illustrated catalogs. Titles include: GAZEBOS AND GARDEN STRUCTURES ($7.95); BRIDGES AND CUPOLAS ($7.95); BACKYARD STRUCTURES ($8.95); and THE PRIVY ($7.95). You can order any of the books from Sun Designs, P.O. Box 206, Delafield, WI 53018. Include $1.50 for postage and handling. — DJB

Is a Mail·Order Plan Right for You?

Although all the designers and plan services reviewed offer complete construction drawings, those drawings are usually made to conform with national standards. You might have to have them adapted for your climate conditions and for special requirements of your local building department and zoning laws.

In all cases, you'll need to have the house sited on your property and a site plan prepared with proper provisions for utilities, septic system, drainage, drives and entrances, landscaping and views. It's always a good idea to consult with a local construction engineer or architect and your building department engineers before ordering plans.

If you can't find a mail-order plan that's just right; if you find that you're selecting a house that's larger than you need; if your property is steeply sloped; if you have dramatic views that you want to take advantage of, or, if you have special space or site requirements (a darkroom, a pool, a greenhouse or access for someone in a wheelchair, for example), you should consider having a custom home designed. Plan on spending somewhere around 10% of the construction cost for the design fees, allow a few months design time before building and follow the advice on how to select an architect on the next pages. — DJB

Do You Need an Architect?

From the 1856 book,
VILLAGE & FARM
COTTAGES

It is an error to suppose that the architect's aid is needed only by those who erect large and expensive houses. The man who in building is compelled to a close economy has, perhaps, even greater occasion for the best professional advice. The architect who is called to plan such a house, and who would make it suitable and satisfactory, must perform a very important duty before he begins to make a drawing. He certainly cannot adapt his plan to the requirements of his employer, until he has ascertained what those requirements are. But so vague, often are the notions of men, that this is no easy matter. They need help to understand and define their own ideas and wishes. In such cases, the architect must explain, and question, and suggest, until his client, as well as himself, shall have a definite notion in regard to the size, accommodation, style, and cost of the proposed erection, and of those paramount considerations to which every thing else must conform. In this matter of advising, an honorable architect will feel his moral responsibility; consulting not so much his own fancy, as the character and true interest of those who are to occupy the dwelling. It will be his aim so to adapt the house to the habits, needs, and circumstances of the family; so to arrange the whole in respect of eonomy, consistency, and architectural propriety, that the result shall be not only pleasing at first, but from year to year more and more satisfactory.

How to Deal With
Your Architect

♦ ♦ ♦ ♦ ♦

To the selection of a proper architect must be devoted all the experience of a lifetime of observation of men and works. That large class of humble strivers after the right which, for convenience, is broadly designated as the laity, feel their own dependence and inferiority before the professional man, and stand a little in awe of his knowledge, as well as of that adjustable code known as professional etiquette. Throw away such thoughts and regard him not as a superior, to be delicately handled, but as a man whose duty and pleasure it is to serve you.

It is safe to assume that a woman who has kept house intelligently for ten years knows more than any architect about the best practical arrangement of rooms for her family. On that point she should not be too self-effacing.

From THE HOUSE & HOME, 1897

BUILDING YOUR HOME

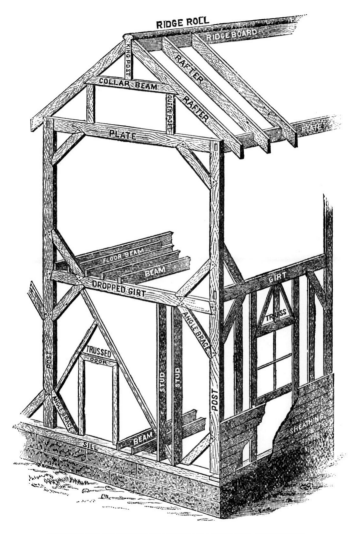

BRACED FRAME SHOWING NAMES OF TIMBERS, SHEATHING
TRUSSED WINDOW, ETC.

Three Rules for Homebuilders

❖ ❖ ❖ ❖ ❖

The following, which are a few of the rules to be observed in building houses, may afford some useful suggestions to those about to engage in such undertakings.

1. Always compare the *cost* with the *means*, before deciding on the plan. It is much better to build within means, than to have a large, fine house, hard to keep in order, and encumbering the owner with a heavy and annoying debt. A great error with many is an attempt to build *finely*. Attend to *real* wants and substantial convenience, and avoid imaginary and manufactured desires.

2. Study a convenient location rather than a showy one: a house on a lofty hill may make a fine appearance, but the annoyance of ascending to it will become greater on each successive day.

3. Build of such good materials as are near at hand. With great economy over the use of such as are "far brought and dear bought."

❖ ❖ ❖ ❖ ❖

From THE REGISTER OF RURAL AFFAIRS, 1856

How Much Will Your New House Cost?

From
COTTAGES
AND FARM
HOUSES
1867

A simple and rapid plan for estimating the cost of any building is by comparison. If carefully done, it will give figures that may be relied on. We will suppose that a party desires to erect a building. Let him select such a house already built in that vicinity as shall represent, in style of architecture and character of finish, about what he desires to construct, and of which the cost of building is known; then compute the area or number of square feet covered by the building; divide the number of dollars of cost by the number of square feet thus found, and the price per square foot is ascertained.

Thus a house 40 feet by 40 feet covers an area of 1,600 square feet; it costs $8,000; and dividing $8,000 by 1,600, shows $5 per square foot. Now what will be the cost of a similar house covering 1,400 square feet? 1,400 x $5 = $7,000.

This plan will do very well to approximate roughly to cost. A better and closer one is to ascertain the cost per cubic foot. Thus, a house 40 feet by 40 feet, and an average height of 30 feet. 40 x 40 x 30 = 48,000 cubic feet, cost $7,200, or fifteen cents per cubic feet. Then a house containing 57,000 cubic feet, at fifteen cents, would cost $8,550. Where all conditions of comparison are equal, such as equal facilities for buying, equal advantages in capital, credit, good management, etc., one can very closely by, this last method, ascertain about the cost of such a building as he proposes to erect.

Can You Build a House?

◆ ◆ ◆ ◆ ◆

Most men in America, who build country houses, are their own "Clerk of the Works," that is to say, they undertake to supply the materials, and employ the mechanics; they mostly plan the building, and they take all the general superintendence of the labor. And a sorry time they have of it! If it strengthens patriotism to fight battles for one's country, our amateur builders ought to have a patriotic attachment to their country homes, for many of them have a sore conflict of mind and body from the time they commence building till they bid a joyful adieu to the house-painter.

It does not require much observation to discover the reason of all this difficulty and perplexity. To state it plainly, it is nothing more nor less than the ignorance of the proprietor himself of the whole art of building. Every man does not fancy that he can make a coat, or weave a tapestry, without instruction—yet every man is quite certain that he can not only build a house, but build a much better one, in many respects, than he has seen before, *till he has tried!*

By A. J. Downing, from his HINTS TO PERSONS ABOUT BUILDING IN THE COUNTRY, 1847

How to Fix Construction Costs

The Final Bill

The cost of the proposed work is like the algebraic x, an unknown quantity, unless one of two methods is adopted— and they are open to adverse criticism. To sell a house for thirty thousand dollars one must ask thirty-five for it; to build a house for a prescribed sum one must name to the architect twenty per cent less. It is quite impossible to determine whether it is the ambition of the architect, or the extravagance of his client, or the unstable scale of prices for either labor or materials, which makes this a truism; but certain it is that no one ever yet built within his first-named sum. If time were plenty and years did not count, it could be possible to use the other method of keeping within a certain amount. The architect would then finish his drawings and specifications, from excavations to brass keys, and draw and sign all contracts. Then, by adding the amounts, he would know the entire necessary expenditure. This sounds simple, but experiment has proved it to be almost impracticable, as well as unsatisfactory to the owner, for it makes changes impossible, and few know from drawings what the completed structure will be.

From THE HOUSE & HOME, 1897

The Building Department

* * * * *

Where the building to be erected is within the jurisdiction of a municipal or State Building Department, it is best to have the plans approved by the department before awarding the contract. This precaution will cost nothing, and may save charges for extra work. If such a clause as the following, "All work must be done in accordance with the requirements of the Department of Buildings, and any changes in the work made by the order of said department will form a part of this contract, and will be done by the contractor without cost to the owner," is relied upon to protect the owner, he may rest assured that the contractor will make due allowance in his estimate price for all possibilities, and take the benefit of any doubt, when in fact there need be no doubt.

From HOW TO BUILD A HOME, 1897

Build by Contract

Late to Work

◆ ◆ ◆ ◆ ◆

A good deal of observation and experience has convinced us that building *by contract* is, in nearly all cases, the better mode in this country. If your master-workman is a man of integrity, he will serve you as faithfully under a fair contract as by the day's-work system, and, if he is not, there is even more likelihood of your being cheated in the latter case than in the former. Letting the work under contract, makes the contractor the only accountable person, and your own supervision is confined to observing that he fulfils the conditions of his contract; and rids you, besides, of the trouble of watching a dozen or twenty subordinates.

There is an opinion strongly maintained by some (and for the indulgence of which they are willing to pay dearly), that good workmanship can only come by the *day's-work* system. We have not found, on comparison of houses built in the different modes, that there is any practical truth in it. Everything, as we have said, depends on the master-workman, and, in this country, if he is allowed a fair compensation for the "job," we believe as much justice is always done in one case as the other.

By A. J. Downing, from his HINTS TO PERSONS ABOUT BUILDING IN THE COUNTRY, 1847

The Building Contract

Let no one persuade you to make separate contracts with various contractors—builder, plumber, mason, etc. Unless there is one responsible contractor for the whole work, each of the contractors will plead negligence on the part of one or more of the rest as an excuse for delays. The builder will insist that the mason did not get his foundations finished in time; the plasterer will insist that the roofer did not finish in time for him to commence his work with necessary protection against the weather, etc. Moreover,—and this is a serious matter,—any injury to the building by reason of neglect to protect against the elements will be a matter for which an owner who has various contractors will alone be responsible, whereas if he has one contractor, under obligation to finish and deliver the building in good condition, he will be relieved of protecting the building from storms, washouts, etc., and will also be relieved of the expense of paying watchmen for nights and holidays.

Plenty of time should be given to the various estimating contractors to make their figures, and money will be lost if they are required to estimate without sufficient time for investigation.

From the 1897 book, HOW TO BUILD A HOME

Let Your Builder Know What You Want

It is not enough that he who proposes to build should have fully planned the structure, and that all its particulars are distinctly fixed in his own mind. This plan must be made equally clear to the mechanics who are to execute it. It should be so plain as to leave no chance for misunderstanding or perversion. And this requires that all the parts which can be so represented should be shown by drawings made to a scale sufficiently large to admit of measurement by the workmen. Every thing of importance for them to know, which cannot be drawn, should be fully described in writing. Floor-plans, showing the position and dimensions of walls and partitions; elevations, giving the form of each side, with the windows, doors, and other details; framing plans, determining the size and place of each stick of timber to be used; sections of mouldings, cornices, stairs, and all those parts which are of irregular outline; the whole accompanied by careful specifications of the quality of all materials, and the manner of their use,—are not only necessary in order to estimate, before building, what it will cost, but form the surest safeguard against misunderstandings, and against the taking of wrongful advantage when work is done by contract.

From the 1856 book, VILLAGE & FARM COTTAGES

Build With Wood

A difference of opinion has, and probably always will exist about the materials of which a house should be constructed. We use in this country three leading varieties, wood, brick, and stone, and, to a limited extent, grout and iron. Wood is the cheapest, and if very nice points are considered, is probably the healthiest, certainly the driest. Frame houses have also superior qualities for ventilation, a subject very little understood by those who advocate imprenetrable walls and double windows. So little progress has been made in understanding the subject of ventilation, that the commissioners, in advertising for plans for the new Capitol building for the State of New York, mention the necessity of open fire-places for this purpose. Our stone and brick houses, with slate and metal roofs, furnace-heated and air-tight, lack essential qualities for health; while a frame-house, which admits the air more freely, even if it take an extra cord or two of wood, or an extra supply of coal, has a more healthy atmosphere.

From the 1867 book, COTTAGES AND FARM HOUSES

Poor Construction

Homebuilding Hints

In building, cheapness is not always true economy. To build without a reasonable regard for strength and durability, merely for the sake of saving, evinces but a short-sighted frugality.

The question of economy is not a simple geometrical problem, as some would have us consider it. It is not difficult to decide what form of structure will give, with the least amount of material, and at the lowest cost of erection, the greatest quantity of cubic space. Leaving out of the question looks and convenience, the rule might do for a temporary barn, which is to hold nothing but hay; and this is about the extent of its application.

◆ ◆ ◆

Spare no pains to obtain the services of honest, intelligent master-mechanics, as deficiencies of construction and execution, and heavy bills of extras, are more frequently the result of dull incapacity and stupid neglect than of a grasping disposition, or of a willful intention to deceive.

By Calvert Vaux, from his 1867 book, VILLAS & COTTAGES

Economy in Homebuilding

◆ ◆ ◆ ◆ ◆

The top soil is valuable, and should be carefully removed to one side (where it will not be in the way, necessitating subsequent removal), to be readjusted upon the terraces or other surfaces for support of grass, flowers, and other vegetation. It is often foolishly mixed up with the clay and sand, necessitating the purchase afterward of good soil when top dressing is necessary.

From HOW TO BUILD A HOME, 1897

◆ ◆ ◆

If the purse is small, let the necessary economy be confined to the elimination of ornament, but never let it tempt the builder to slight the construction of the house. Where there is a choice between showiness and worth, put effect aside, and aim first of all to have the house well constructed of durable, but not extravagant, materials.

From THE HOUSE & HOME, 1897

Building Hints

Pine is undoubtedly a better material than hemlock, yet the latter is much cheaper, and, if of fair quality, is nearly as good for constructive purposes as pine. It is, therefore, quite sufficient in all ordinary buildings to construct the frame, joists, partitions, and roofs of hemlock, using clear pine for the external and internal fittings and finish. Oak is the best, and, in the end, the most economical material to use for heavy timber across wide openings. Chestnut, in short lengths and well supported, is well suited for rough joists or sleepers required for boarded floors close to the earth; and locust-wood, though costly, is invaluable in moist situations for any posts, furring strips, or other wood-work that comes in direct connection with damp basement walls.

◆ ◆ ◆

A point that requires much attention in the study of details is, to *make the ornament secondary to the construction, and not the construction secondary to the ornament.* This is the fatal rock on which so many a good conception for a house has been split. An inexperienced man, for example, may conclude to have an ornamental plaster-ceiling in his parlor, and in his desire to have it good of its sort, he may so load it down with decoration that it will be much more disagreeable to look at than the plain ceiling was before it was touched. And so it is throughout the whole subject of domestic architecture: *it is always as easy to spoil a house by overdoing it as by underdoing it.*

By Calvert Vaux, from his 1867 book, VILLAS & COTTAGES

When the Building Starts

◆ ◆ ◆ ◆ ◆

The scene around buildings in the process of erection is often very disorderly. This may be prevented by a little timely precaution. Let the owner designate, beforehand, places where the various materials shall be deposited, and mark out such space as may be needed for doing the work. The remaining part of the grounds and the trees, if it contain them, may be protected from injury, by a temporary fence. In his agreement with the builder, he should have a provision making him responsible for any damage that may accrue to his own or his neighbor's property through the carelessness or rudeness of the workmen.

Persons unaccustomed to watch the progress of a building, are liable to be deceived by its appearance in the earlier stages. The rooms look small and seem to be growing smaller, and very few things appear as they supposed they would. Hence often, needless apprehensions and worse than needless complaints. To such, we can only say that they are not competent judges in the case. All that they can do is patiently to await the completion of the structure. By that time, in all probability, their trouble and fears will have vanished.

From the 1856 book, VILLAGE & FARM COTTAGES

FINISHES & FURNISHINGS

❖ ❖ ◆ ❖ ❖

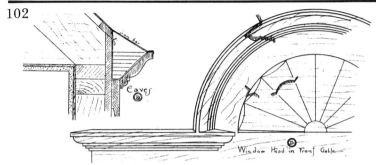

Eaves

Window Head in Front Gable

The Construction Details

The owner should require the architect to furnish details of the trim (by which is meant the wood finish, window-frames, door-frames, wash- or base-boards, panels under windows, wainscoting, etc.) promptly,—in fact, simultaneously with the plans and other specifications,—in order that the builder may have no excuse for not having all of the trim kiln-dried in time for finishing the building.

This is a more important matter than at first glance it may appear to be. Builders and contractors are often prevented from finishing their work in time through the negligence of architects in furnishing details, drawings, etc., and do not like to put the blame where it belongs; no builder likes to quarrel with an influential architect. In the accompanying contract with the architect this has been provided for, and the owner should see that all of the working plans, details, drawings, etc., are fully completed before taking an estimate for the work. He will thus get better prices, because each contractor will know exactly what he has to do, and will not make undue allowance for construction details as to which he may have to guess.

The owner, too, will find it advisable to go over the drawings of the standing trim, doors, patterns of the main staircase, etc., as in case they do not suit him it will be too late to remedy the matter after they have been prepared and brought to the building.

Do not, under any circumstances, consent to have your architect take estimates with the indefinite clause, "Details hereafter to be furnished."

From HOW TO BUILD A HOME, 1897

Avoid the Gewgawgery

♦ ♦ ♦ ♦ ♦

The work should be simple, because cheaper in the first place, in construction, and finish; quite as appropriate and satisfactory in appearance; and demanding infinitely less labor and pains to care for, and protect it afterward. Therefore all mouldings, architraves, chisel-work, and gewgawgery in interior finish should be let alone in the living and daily occupied rooms of the house. If, to a single parlor, or spare bedchamber a little ornamental work be permitted, let even that be in moderation, and just enough to teach the active mistress and her daughters what a world of scrubbing and elbow work they have saved themselves in the enjoyment of a plainly-finished house, instead of one full of gingerbread work and finery.

From the 1852 book, RURAL ARCHITECTURE, by Lewis A. Allen

Making Shingles

The Wood Shingle Roof

• • ◆ • •

For covering roofs of houses in the country there is scarcely any good material so generally available as shingles, if the pitch is not too flat. The great advantage of a shingle roof is, that it is scarcely possible for it to get out of order till the wood absolutely rots; and this takes many years to accomplish if the shingles are tolerable and the work well done. It also allows of considerable expansion, contraction, and even settlement, without the slightest injury to its efficiency. It is agreeably varied in surface, and assumes, by age, a soft, pleasant, neutral tint that harmonizes with any color that may be used in the building. A shingle roof in cities, or even closely-built villages, is objectionable in case of fire, because the loose, lighted chips from an adjacent burning building will be likely to inflame it. But this objection does not amount to much in a detached building in the country.

By E. H. Leland, from his 1882 book, FARM COTTAGES

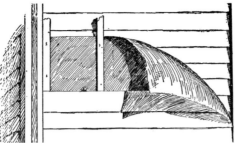

Re-siding an old wall.

Wood Siding

The ordinary mode of horizontal siding seems preferable in most situations. It offers a simple, fair surface, that can be broadly treated both in form and color, for the slight projection of one board over the other does not give sufficient variety of light and shade to interfere with the general effect as a whole. Another method is to groove and tongue the boards together, and bring all to one smooth surface. This plan has nothing to recommend it; it is more costly, more likely to get out of order by expansion and contraction, and is scarcely more agreeable in appearance. It is possible, instead of using siding, to cover a building with shingles, and to cut them into ornamental patterns. And this was often done by the Dutch settlers; but the projection is so slight, that not much additional effect is gained, except, perhaps, in quite small buildings, for the impression that a residence of tolerable size makes on the eye depends very little on such merely superficial detail.

Another plan is to use vertical boarding, with battens to cover the joints, for an external covering. This mode has some advantages, and its appearance is often preferred. It is well suited for barns or small buildings, where the battens are relatively large enough to form part of the design; but when used on a larger scale, it is apt to give a striped, liny appearance to a house that injures its broad, general effect, and to draw particular attention to the fact that it is built of wood. This fact should not in any way be denied; but it is not desirable to make it especially prominent, as if it was something to be particularly proud of.

From the 1867 book, VILLAS & COTTAGES

Don't Paint Your House White

It seems almost unnecessary to allude to the custom of painting houses white, but the practice is yet continued with pertinacity, as if the highest idea of beauty was reached in a white house with green blinds. Riding along our village and country roads, white houses, reflecting the rays of a bright sun, will glare at us on every side, until the sense is absolutely pained, and relief is sought by closing the eyes. These places are often without a particle of shade of trees or vines. To be sure, it takes time to raise trees, but many of the houses could be absolutely transformed by the expenditure of a single dollar for climbing vines, and affording them the proper care in raising and training them. It makes no difference with the seasons in regard to white houses, for if the sun shines less brightly or is obscured by clouds in winter, it is probable that, at the north, the ground will be covered with snow, between which and the house there is no contrast, but all is an unbroken field of white. There is no excuse for such shocking displays of bad taste, and with all the attention that is being given to art by our young people, it is to be hoped that this feature of our early development will soon be lost.

From VICK'S MONTHLY MAGAZINE, 1881

Follow Nature's Color Scheme

No one is successful in rural improvements, who does not study nature, and take her for the basis of his practice. Now, in natural landscape, any thing like strong and bright colours is seldom seen, except in very minute portions, and least of all pure white—chiefly appearing in small objects like flowers. The practical rule which should be deduced from this, is, to avoid all these colours which nature avoids. In buildings, we should copy those that she offers chiefly to the eye—such as those of the soil, rocks, wood, and the bark of trees,—the materials of which houses are built. These materials offer us the best and most natural study from which harmonious colours for the houses themselves should be taken.

Country houses, thickly surrounded by trees, should always be painted of a lighter shade than those standing exposed. And a new house, entirely unrelieved by foliage, as it is rendered conspicuous by the very nakedness of its position, should be painted several shades darker than the same building if placed in a well wooded site. *In proportion as a house is exposed to view, let its hue be darker, and where it is much concealed by foliage, a very light shade of colour is to be preferred.*

From THE HORTICULTURIST 1847

Painting Your Country Home

The question of color is a most interesting one in any design for a country house, and seems at present but little understood in America, by far the greater number of houses being simply painted white, with bright green blinds. By this means each residence is distinctly protruded from the surrounding scenery, and instead of grouping and harmonizing with it, asserts a right to carry on a separate business on its own account; and this lack of sympathy between the building and its surroundings is very disagreeable to an artistic eye. Even a harsh, vulgar outline may often pass without particular notice in a view of rural scenery, if the mass is quiet and harmonious in color; while a very tolerable composition may injure materially the views near it if it is painted white, the human eye being so constituted that it will be constantly held in bondage by this striking blot of crude light, and compelled to give it unwilling attention.

In some cases, the house-painters themselves show a laudable desire to escape from monotonous repetition; but, on the other hand, they are often very troublesome opponents to reform in this matter. And this is not to be wondered at; for a mechanic who has been brought up on a chalk-white and spinach-green diet ever since he was old enough to handle a brush, can hardly help having but little taste for delicate variety, because a perpetual contemplation of white lead and verdigris is calculated to have the same effect on the eye that incessant tobacco-chewing has on the palate: in each case the organ is rendered incapable of nice appreciation.

From the 1867 book, VILLAS & COTTAGES, by Calvert Vaux

Interior Woodwork

For door and window trims and other interior woodwork, white pine is recommended, as it is the cheapest, and, if properly finished, looks very well. It may be stained, if too light—the transparent stains merely darken the wood and do not conceal the natural grain. Under no circumstances try to imitate oak or walnut by graining. Such shams deceive no one and are in the worst taste. If we use paint for interior work let us use it frankly, carefully selecting the color, and avoiding a shiny surface, a flatted or dull finish being preferable.

◆ ◆ ◆

The interior wood-work should be selected with some little care, and all stained—either satin-wood or light black-walnut. These stains, which can be easily procured, are better if laid on in oil, and then, if covered with two coats of varnish, make the nearest approach possible to the appearance of the above-named natural woods. No grainer's art can do as well. Handsomely stained and varnished wood-work is, we think, the most superior mode of treating interiors. It adds much to the warmth and cosiness of the rooms, has the effect of furnishing, and, so far as cleanliness is concerned, is of great help to the housekeeper. This style of finish, whether for the humble cottage or costly mansion, is better and more attractive, if done with good taste, than the most costly and elaborately painted tints.

From the 1884 book, COTTAGES OR HINTS ON ECONOMICAL BUILDING

Wainscoting

◆ ◆ ◆ ◆ ◆

Someday, when you have nothing better to do, take a yardstick through your house and measure the height, above the floor, of all the finger marks, dents and chipped paint on your walls. You'll find that over 90% of them are lower than that yardstick and you'll have discovered why last century's homeowners loved wainscoting.

Any type of wood, stained a natural color and capped between three and four feet high with a "chair-rail," would protect halls, staircases, kitchens and any other well used room. The illustration above, of an 1881 dining room, shows how the chair-rail keeps the weight of a heavy sideboard off the soft plaster wall. — DJB

The Value of Old Furniture

We have a decided penchant for all that smacks of antiquity. We like old houses and old furniture, particularly if comely and serviceable. We delight in painting to ourselves the scenes through which they must have passed; we believe, too, that they exert a much greater influence in producing a love for home than those constructed at a more recent period.

We would gladly see the money now expended in the trashy, half-made articles of furniture, merely because the uncomfortable shapes of some of them are said to be of the latest style, laid out for those which are truly strong and serviceable, and, for this reason, elegant.

From WOODWARD'S COTTAGES AND FARM HOUSES, 1867

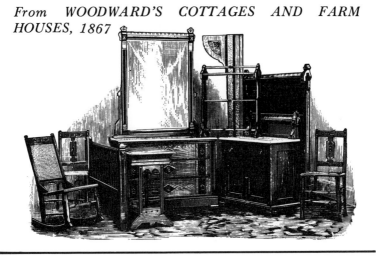

Houseplants

◆ ◆ ◆ ◆ ◆

Plants, whether upon a stand or hanging in appropriate pots at the window, add amazingly to the cheerfulness of any room, contributing to the pleasure of those who care and tend for them. They serve also as useful barometers, telling us, by their condition, of the atmospherical state of our apartments, their delicate organization being unable to stand against the injurious emanation from overheated furnaces. Mr. Rand, in his pleasant book upon flowers, says, A plant or a stand of flowers is a constant source of pleasure in a room; it is a spring of sunshine, and its silent influence makes all the household more cheerful and better.

From WOODWARD'S COTTAGES AND FARM HOUSES, 1867

LANDSCAPING
YOUR COUNTRY HOME

A Country Home Design Should Never Be Finished

❖ ❖ ❖ ❖ ❖

It is a mistake to aim at the completion of a country home in a season, or in two, or some half a dozen. Its attractiveness lies, or should lie, in its prospective growth of charms. Your city home—when once the architect, and plumber, and upholsterer have done their work—is in a sense complete, and the added charms must lie in the genial socialities and hospitalities with which you can invest it; but with a country home, the fields, the flowers, the paths, the hundred rural embellishments, may be made to develop a constantly recurring succession of attractive features. This year, a new thicket of shrubbery, or a new gate-way on some foot-path; next year, the investment of some out-lying ledge with floral wonders; the season after may come the establishment of a meadow (by judicious drainage) where some ugly marsh has offended the eye; and the succeeding summer may show the redemption of the harsh briary up-land that you have scourged into fertility and greenness.

By Donald G. Mitchel, from his 1867 book, RURAL STUDIES

Country Home Essentials

The additions of porches, verandas, bay-windows, etc., increase the effect of cottage-houses to a very considerable degree, add much to interior convenience and beauty, and, if put on at the time when the building is constructed, do not materially augment the expense. We think they are always worth their full cost, and rarely fail to make an impression upon the eye of a purchaser.

The place designed simply for a summer residence for the citizen, who is obliged to be at his office or counting room daily, bating the few weeks of summer vacation, need not be so complete in its appointments and arrangements, as the permanent country residence. One essential condition, however, in this case is, that there shall be *room enough*, with ample verandahs, and shaded gravel walks, which will afford opportunities for open air exercise in all states of the weather. There is nothing, perhaps, that interferes so essentially with the citizen's enjoyment of the country, as the want of facilities for out door exercise. It is too hot or too dusty to ride or walk, before the shower, and after its refreshment has come, it is wet and muddy. Build spacious verandahs, shaded with vines, and well-made walks, always firm and dry, bordered with shrubbery, or overhung with trees.

From COTTAGES AND FARM HOUSES, 1867

A Good Investment

There is a grand error which many fall into in building, looking as they do only at the extent of wood and timber, or stone and mortar in the structure, and paying no attention to the surroundings, which in most cases contribute more to the effect of the establishment than the structure itself, and which, if uncultivated or neglected, any amount of expenditure in building will fail to give that completeness and perfection of character which every homestead should command.

Trees properly distributed, give a value to an estate far beyond the cost of planting, and tending their growth, and which no other equal amount of labor and expense upon it can confer. Innumerable farms and places have been sold at high prices, over those of perhaps greater producing value, merely for the trees which embellished them. Thus, in a pecuniary light, to say nothing of the pleasure and luxury they confer, trees are a source of profitable investment.

If the planter feels disposed to consult authorities, as to the best disposition of his trees, works on Landscape Gardening may be studied; but these can give only general hints, and the only true course is to strive to make his grounds look as much like nature herself as possible—for nature seldom makes mistakes in her designs.

From the 1852 book, RURAL ARCHITECTURE, by Lewis A. Allen

A Common Mistake

It is not an uncommon spectacle to see a country house built at a lavish expenditure, and in a very ornate style, but placed in the midst of grounds badly laid out and wretchedly kept. The proprietor has exhausted all his forced stock of enthusiasm, and spent all his surplus capital upon his villa, in his architectural *fever*, and his grounds are doomed to suffer the succeeding *ague* of indifference and neglect. A wise man, when he plans a country residence, will so apportion his means that his house may not be out of keeping with his grounds. The same style, the same feeling, should pervade both, and be reflected from one to the other.

From HINTS TO PERSONS ABOUT BUILDING IN THE COUNTRY, 1847

Make Your Home
a Part of the Landscape

◆ ◆ ◆ ◆ ◆

A farm with its buildings, or a simple country residence with the grounds which enclose it, or a cottage with its door-yard and garden, should be finished sections of the landscape of which it forms a part. A dwelling house, no matter what the style, standing alone, either on hill or plain, apart from other objects, would hardly be an attractive sight. As a mere representation of a particular style of architecture, or as a model of imitation, it might excite our admiration, but it would not be an object on which the eye and the imagination could repose with satisfaction.

But assemble around that dwelling subordinate structures, trees, and shrubbery properly disposed, and it becomes an object of exceeding interest and pleasure in the contemplation.

From the 1852 book, RURAL ARCHITECTURE, by Lewis A. Allen

Landscape Design

The beauty of a cottage or villa, like all beauty of a higher kind, is, we think, much enhanced by a due concealment, rather than a bold display of its attractions. Gleaming through a veil of soft green foliage, we are led to magnify its charms, from there being something pleasing suggested, which is not seen. If, on the contrary, we see the whole building studiously exposed, and that but too often in the broad sunshine, we are only inclined to turn away in disappointment.

By A. J. Downing, from his HINTS TO PERSONS ABOUT BUILDING IN THE COUNTRY, 1847

Decorate With Vines

Beautiful are the ways of the Vine, whether it be the bold and vigorous Virginia Creeper, that finds foothold on the most forbidding wall, and grows the stronger and greater for the winds and storms that beat upon it, or the light and delicate Smilax, weaving its emerald-green tracery across the window panes, or around the portraits of beloved friends.

The forests are full of beautiful vines. Convolvulus, Bitter Sweet, Scarlet, and Yellow Honeysuckle, Virgin's Bower, Grape, and other graceful wild climbers, are within the reach of almost every country house, and should be sought after and wooed to grow around porches, and over gateways, and up on the roofs of unlovely sheds.

The Hop is a wholesome, thrifty vine, and if none other could be had, I would gladly and gratefully train it over verandas, and across kitchen and pantry windows, and rejoice in its cool shade and clean fragrance. But whoever has the good luck to live near a bit of wild woodland, can be generally sure of finding many things that will add grace and beauty to the plainest little home.

By E. H. Leland, from his 1882 book, FARM COTTAGES

A PLAIN COUNTRY HOUSE

Let Time Decorate Your Home

Time, in its many changes, adds beauty and value to a country home that is taken care of, whose occupants enjoy and are interested in every tree and shrub, and every improvement that is made. Fruits, flowers, and ornamental foliage develop new attractions; and a little done to-day, and a little to-morrow, while being but healthful recreation, amounts to a good deal at the end of a year.

From the 1867 book, COTTAGES AND FARM HOUSES

THE SAME HOUSE, DECORATED

Country Planting

Most men go to the country to make an easy thing of it. If they must commence study of all the later discoveries in vegetable physiology, and keep a sharp eye upon all new varieties of fruit—lest they fall behind the age; and trench their land every third year, and screen it—may be—in order to ensure the most perfect comminution of the soil, they find themselves entering upon the labors of a new profession, instead of lightening the fatigues of an old one.

Limit yourself, until you have felt your way, to some ten or a dozen of the best established varieties; don't be afraid of old things if they are good; if a gaunt Rhode Island Greening tree is struggling in your hedge-row, trim it, scrape it, soap it, dig about it, pull away the turf from it, lime it, and then if you can keep up a fair fight against the bugs and the worms, you will have fine fruit from it; if you can't, cut it down. If a veteran mossy pear tree is in your door-yard, groom it as you would a horse—just in from a summering in briary pastures.

Save some sheltered spot for a trellis, where you may plant a Delaware, an Iona or two, a Rebecca, and a Diana. Put a Concord at your southside door—its rampant growth will cover your trellised porch in a pair of seasons; it will give you some fine clusters, even though you allow it to tangle; the pomologists will laugh at you; but let them: you will have your shade and the wilderness of frolicsome tendrils, and at least a fair show of purple bunches. Scatter here and there hardy herbaceous flowers that shall care for themselves, and which the children may pluck with a will. Don't distress yourself if your half acre of lawn shows some hummocks, or dandelions, or butter-cups. And if a wild clump of bushes intrude in a corner, don't condemn it too hastily; it may be well to enliven it with an evergreen or two—to dig about it, and paint its edges with a few summer phloxes or roses.

By Donald G. Mitchel, from his 1867 book, RURAL STUDIES

The True Luxuries of a Country Home

♦ ♦ ♦ ♦ ♦

Bringing together all the luxuries which a complete country residence may afford, with all the comforts and conveniences which may be combined in a single place, is of a very rare but by no means difficult attainment. Such a place must comprise, besides the best household conveniences, trees and plants for the entire circle of fruits; a first-rate kitchen garden, for a full supply of the best early, medium and late vegetables; fresh meat and poultry; and lastly, and by no means the least, the wholesome fascinations of ornamental planting. Throwing aside the costly fruits of hot-house culture, all these may be easily had at a moderate expenditure of means.

From THE REGISTER OF RURAL AFFAIRS, 1858

A good house; but the home is only half built.

A house and a home.

From THE FARMSTEAD, 1900, by L.H. Bailey

Good Reading

THE ARCHITECTURE OF COUNTRY HOUSES, by A. J. Downing, a reprint of the 1850 original, 484p, softcover, $7.95 + 85¢ p&h — Dover Publications, 31 East Second St., Mineola, NY 11501

THE BACKYARD HOMESTEAD, MINI FARM & GARDEN LOG BOOK, by John Jeavons, J. Morgodor Griffin & Robin Leler, a record book, calendar and guide to an efficient homestead, 224p, softcover, $8.95 + 1.00 p&h — Ten Speed Press, Box 7123, Berkeley, CA 94707

BEAUTIFYING COUNTRY HOMES, by Jacob Weidenmann, a reprint of the original 1870 landscape guide, 108p, softcover, $9.95 + 2.00 p&h — American Life Foundation, Box 349, Watkins Glen, NY 14891

BEFORE YOU BUILD, a Preconstruction Guide, by Robert Roskind, The Owner Builder Center, a guidebook to choosing a site, evaluating solar potential, providing for utilities, planning drives and understanding codes, permits, financing and insurance, 240 p, softcover, $8.95 + 1.00 p&h — Ten Speed Press, Box 7123, Berkeley, CA 94707

BUILDING YOUR OWN HOUSE, the First Part: From Foundations to Framing, by Robert Roskind, The Owner Builder Center, a clear step-by-step guide to basic building techniques, 448p, $17.95 + 1.00 p&h, Ten Speed Press, Box 7123, Berkeley, CA 94707

CLASSIC OLD HOUSE PLANS, Three Centuries of American Domestic Architecture, by Lawrence Grow, floor plans, elevations and details from original 17th, 18th & 19th century sources, 128p, softcover, $8.95 + 1.50 p&h — The Main Street Press, William Case House, Pittstown, NJ 08867

COTTAGE RESIDENCES, by A.J. Downing, a reprint of the 1842 original, 352p, softcover, $6.95 + 85¢ p&h — Dover Publications, 31 East Second St., Mineola, NY 11501

COUNTRY ARCHITECTURE, by Lawrence Grow, 100 original, 19th century plans, for barns, stables, gazebos, greenhouses, smokehouses, sheds and other outbuildings, 128 p, softcover, $9.95 + 1.50 p&h — The Main Street Press, William Case House, Pittstown, NY 08867

THE COUNTRY GARDENERS ALMANAC, by Martin Lawrence, a complete calendar of gardening chores with practical advice culled from 19th century farm journals, 224p, softcover, $9.95 + 1.50 p&h — The Main Street Press, William Case House, Pittstown, NJ 08867

COUNTRY PATTERNS, A Sampler of 19th Century American Home and Landscape Design, edited by Donald J. Berg, 128 p, softcover, $8.95 + 1.50 p&h — The Main Street Press, William Case House, Pittstown, NJ 08867

COUNTRY WISDOM BULLETINS, ninety-seven different, 32p booklets with practical how-to advice on home energy, food gardening, maintenance, cooking, preserving and old-time crafts — Storey Communications, Schoolhouse Road, Pownal, VT 05261

THE FORGOTTEN ARTS SERIES, five books that explain how to master dozens of old-time household skills — Yankee Inc., Box F, Depot Square, Peterborough, NH 03458

HOMESTEAD HINTS, A compendium of Useful Information from the Past for the Home, Garden and Household, edited by Donald J. Berg, 128p, softcover, $6.95 + 1.00 p&h — Ten Speed Press, Box 7123, Berkeley, CA 94707

HOW TO GET IT BUILT, Better, Faster and for Less, by Werner R. Hashagen, a complete guide through the construction process, 242p, softcover, $18.00 + 2.00 p&h — Werner R. Hashagen, Architect, 7480 La Jolla Blvd., La Jolla, CA 92037

MORE CLASSIC OLD HOUSE PLANS, Authentic Designs for Colonial and Victorian Homes, by Lawrence Grow, floor plans, elevations and details for seventy-five traditional homes, 128p, softcover, $8.95 + 1.50 p&h — The Main Street Press, William Case House, Pittstown, NJ 08867

THE VEGETABLE GARDEN, by MM. Vilmorin-Andrieux, a reprint of the 1885 original, 620p, softcover, $11.95 + 1.00 p&h— Ten Speed Press, Box 7123, Berkeley, CA 94707

VILLAGE & FARM COTTAGES, by Cleveland & Backus, a reprint of the 1856 home plan "pattern" book and builders guide, 189p, softcover, $6.95 + 2.00 p&h — American Life Foundation, Box 349, Watkins Glen, NY 14891

VILLAS & COTTAGES, by Calvert Vaux, a reprint of the 1857 original, 348p, softcover, $6.50 + 85¢ p&h — Dover Publications, 31 East Second St., Mineola, NY 11501

INDEX

◆ ◆ ◆ ◆ ◆

Donald Berg, an architect, lives and works in Rockville Centre, New York. His column, HOMESTEAD HINTS, appears in newspapers across the country. He collected the hints for this book while designing a country home, pond and landscape in southern Vermont.